crafting
frames
at home

COUNTRY LIVING

crafting frames at home

Text by Vitta Poplar
Photography by Keith Scott Morton
Styling by Amy Leonard

HEARST BOOKS

A Division of Sterling Publishing Co., Inc.

NEW YORK

This book was previously published as a hardcover under the title
Country Living Handmade Frames: Decorative Accents for Your Home

Produced by Smallwood & Stewart, Inc., New York City
Editor: Carrie Chase
Art Director: Debbie Sfetsios
Designer: Alexandra Maldonado

Library of Congress Cataloging-in-Publication Data
Available upon request.

10 9 8 7 6 5 4 3 2 1

First paperback edition 2003
Published by Hearst Books
A Division of Sterling Publishing Co., Inc.
387 Park Avenue South, New York, NY 10016

Country Living and Hearst Books are trademarks
owned by Hearst Magazines Property, Inc., in USA,
and Hearst Communications, Inc., in Canada.

www.countryliving.com

Distributed in Canada by Sterling Publishing
c/o Canadian Manda Group, One Atlantic Avenue, Suite 105
Toronto, Ontario, Canada M6K 3E7
Distributed in Australia by Capricorn Link (Australia) Pty. Ltd.
P.O. Box 704, Windsor, NSW 2756 Australia

Text set in Galliard

Manufactured in Singapore

ISBN 1-58816-288-5

table of **contents**

foreword

For as long as I can remember, I have been a collector of frames. I have found wonderful vintage frames in local antique shops—leaving many in their natural state, having others restored. I have discovered playful, quirky frames at flea markets and garage sales, and ingenious, handmade frames at craft shows throughout the country.

The appeal for me is not only the border variations that frames provide, but also the details they bring to a room. They can be mixed and matched, grouped as a series, or hung individually. They can be inconspicuous on a night table, or become a major focal point in a room. Some are interesting enough to hang without artwork—becoming art themselves.

While a frame and its image are personal choices, there are guidelines that can help you show them off to best advantage. In this book, you will see frames hanging in many different kinds of rooms and spaces, and learn some of the principles of how framed pictures work. Pairing a frame with a mat, looking beyond the world of prints for other framing possibilities, and creating *tableaux*—displaying framed images with other complementary objects—are just a few of the many topics explored. There are also more than a dozen original framing projects, which I hope will inspire your creativity and help you to see beyond standard frame offerings.

— Nancy Mernit Soriano, Editor in Chief

introduction

Putting a frame around a picture or an object lends it a certain presence. We are all familiar with the way that ornate frames in museums and galleries add to the power of a work of art. Once singled out and paired with the right frame and mat, even the humblest subject—a pressed flower, an old ticket stub, a leaf—can take on a new beauty, while the most sentimental—an old family letter, a time-worn woolen child's mitten—is preserved and kept on display.

Just as the right frame can transform a subject, so a beautifully framed picture can transform a room. A single well-framed image, or a grouping of several, is one of the easiest and quickest ways to improve the look and feel of any space, creating interest or character where perhaps there was none, highlighting an architectural feature, or even making a room feel larger or smaller.

Making the match between image, mat, and frame—indeed, selecting the image in the first place—is one of the creative joys of framing. In the best examples, of course, there is a harmony not only between the subject and the way in which it is framed but also where and how the picture is hung. Today, there is not a single predominant style of framing—our choice of frames is as diverse as the subjects we select. This book is about finding your style or styles and discovering the pleasure in using frames decoratively throughout the house.

chapter one

what to frame

Maybe you don't think of yourself as a collector, but chances are you've been amassing a lifetime cache without even realizing it. If you have a drawer, closet, or box filled with memorabilia, you probably qualify. And most of it can be framed. Think beyond tradition and see the possibilities in your personal archives: an old letter from your grandmother, pages from a pressed flower album, some colorful buttons from a child's sweater, your favorite baseball player's autograph, a treasured illustration from a 19th-century novel, a prewar road map, or bird feathers gathered on a spring stroll.

In this chapter, we explore the world of collectibles to frame, which includes traditional pictorial images as well as found delights, the occasional odd piece, textiles, and heirloom photographs. As you set out to find new things to frame, keep in mind that much of what you choose will come from your memories, your travels, your interests, your personal history. It might be an image you have long valued, or something that catches your eye as you are out exploring. Whatever draws you to an image—whether it is sentiment or an interest in building a collection—the rewards from framing it well can be great.

Not everything you choose to frame has to be flat. With shadow box frames—deep-backed frames that allow for the display of three-dimensional objects—everyday mementoes once consigned to the attic trunk are candidates for home decor. Grandmother's old glasses and grandfather's pipes, sterling silver baby cups, model boats, antique tools, fishing lures, artists' pens, old coins, seashells, door keys—these all bear witness to the past while enlivening the present. Not only are you putting your memorabilia on display, you are also preserving them for posterity.

Paintings

Even on a limited budget, it is possible to amass an impressive collection of paintings. Generally, unsigned works are more affordable than signed pieces. The same is true for repaired or restored works, which might deter a serious collector but can be quite beautiful. Even seasoned collectors know that buying solely for investment purposes can be risky, as markets fluctuate and are difficult to predict. Instead, listen to your heart—especially if it's easy on your pocketbook. It could even pay off investment-wise. For instance, at one time Victorian paintings with ornate gilt frames

were considered outmoded and went for a song. Primitive American paintings were also undervalued. Not so anymore: Both categories are now out of reach of the casual "Sunday collector." But there are many others to be discovered. If you are seriously interested in buying fine art, consult *Who's Who in American Art*, *Mallett's Index of Artists*, and *Art Prices Current* to determine how much to pay or bid for a signed painting.

But if you don't find an artist's name in a book, don't let that stop you from making a purchase. Keep an open mind: The work of many unsung artists from the past—including grandmothers, art students, and children—regularly appears at flea markets and second-hand shops. Look beyond an unattractive frame, and you might discover a small treasure. Such funky creations might look forlorn sitting alone in the corner of a dusty antique shop, but grouped together and properly framed, they can become part of an intriguing collection.

Living artists are also an important resource. Many savvy collectors snap up the works of not-yet-famous artists before they escalate in value. Consult local newspaper and

The rustic subject matter of this Victorian still-life oil painting dictates its simple wood surround.

The woven trays and baskets on the table in front enhance the picture's folksy effect.

regional magazine listings for open studio tours of artists' workplaces. Visit shows at art schools, galleries (particularly smaller ones in vacation towns, where locals often exhibit their work), and fundraising art shows at historic homes.

As you begin to put together a collection, you might find that you prefer first-rate drawings to second-rate paintings. Drawings can be executed in pencil, charcoal, pen and ink, dry brush, or pastels (which are colored chalks that must be handled with great delicacy). Since pastels can easily be smudged, they must be framed under glass, with a mat to separate them from the glass. This is in marked contrast to oils, which are usually framed without glass.

Printed Matter

A print is broadly defined as anything that comes from a printing press. They are made from one of the following processes:

■ Relief, in which the raised area of a carved surface makes the print. An example is a

woodcut: An image is carved in relief in a block of wood, and is then inked and pressed onto paper. This is printing's earliest form, dating back thousands of years, though many artists still work in the medium today.

■ Intaglio, a process in which the image is cut into a metal plate, the reverse of relief printing. Ink is spread over the plate and absorbed into the cut areas; the rest of the plate is wiped completely clean so that only the cut line prints.

There are several forms of intaglio. With etchings, acid creates the lines of the image in the metal plate and the other areas are protected with an acid-resistant varnish. Repeated immersions in the acid combined with selective applications of varnish create subtle gradations in the final image. Mezzotints (half tones) are produced by scraping and burnishing the metal plate to create tonal effects that are very soft and were especially suited to the reproduction of paintings.

■ Lithography, based on the principle that oil and water repel each other. It involves drawing the image with a grease pencil on a smooth stone, covering with water, then spreading on ink, which clings to the greasy lines. These lines are transferred to paper. The most widespread print form of all—one that served as a news medium before photography—this full-color process was the specialty

In a bedroom with a bed fashioned from baseballs and bats, a collection of simply framed drawings of sports heroes is the natural choice for wall display. On the table below, a bowling pin lamp and a smattering of vintage balls create a sporty tableau.

of Currier and Ives. Popular lithography subjects are landscapes, ship scenes, images of daily life in the countryside, newsworthy events, and politics.

There are contemporary artists who use lithography almost exclusively. Each print is usually signed, often with a notation indicating the total number of prints of the edition as well as the number of that particular print.

Many prints were not originally intended for wall display. They had much more practical applications. Exquisite renderings of tiered Victorian molded custards, "architectural" cakes, and table settings appeared in cookbooks and popular works on etiquette and household management. Architects used books of building design prints as portfolios of completed works. Prints were also a means to share the latest information in the scientific world: For instance, maps of newly explored territories or prints of exotic African bulbs would have been bound together in color-plate books.

In a serene green den, circa 1920 etchings of landscapes, dog pictures, and family portraits line a picture rail and desk. Unlike artwork that is fixed to the walls, these casually propped pieces are meant to be picked up and admired. Each framed image, though part of a group that reflects one family's history, holds its own, due to the harmonious mix of square, rectangular, and oval frame shapes.

Today, original antique prints—as opposed to photographic copies—are priced high, but reproductions are available through catalogs and specialty shops. When determining the value of an original print, know that a remarque—a small artist's drawing or icon often done in pencil or pen—signifies a limited edition and indicates you're dealing with an original (though, alas, forgeries have been printed with premade remarques).

Any reputable dealer or gallery should be able to answer all your questions and provide you with the necessary information about an original print before you make your purchase. However, if you come across what you suspect to be an original print in a bin at auction with no specific information as to its provenance, keep these guidelines in mind. With the intaglio process, you should be able to detect a plate mark on the paper. With the relief process, by contrast, you should see the embossing mark of the printing block. It is just a subtle indentation as compared with the intaglio plate mark, which is a definite depression in the paper indicating where it was pressed against the plate's edge. Also, with

Larger-than-life flowers painted on silk canvas make a strong focal point for an alcove and, hung frame to frame, create **the effect of one image. Though the botanical art tradition is centuries old, artists continue to work in this medium.**

relief prints, the printed line tends to be sharp, while with intaglio prints, it is actually raised. Lithography is the most detailed of all the printing processes, allowing one to record fine nuances of shade and tone; it is by far the most "painterly" of the printing processes. Lithography will not have any of the indentations of the relief and intaglio processes. There could be a slight sheen to the print, and you might detect small bumps created by dust deposits during printing.

You might also come across newer printings made from centuries-old plates. While these are often indistinct and lacking in definition, some collectors overlook these drawbacks if they like the subject matter well enough.

There is no replacement for a trained eye. Frequent print galleries and museums to educate yourself to the qualities and characteristics of fine prints. Whichever type of print you choose to buy, its price tag will not be governed so much by process as by condition, rarity, historical significance, and the prevailing trends of the art market.

Another source of images is drawings from new coffee table books, cut out with a razor blade. On the other hand, book dealers decry the practice of cutting up books old or new, so consider the alternatives. You could use calendar pages, paired with high-quality mats. Clip-art books carry black and white replicas of old prints of flora and fauna. Another possibility is antique seed catalogs, which are thin enough to be framed whole while showing off their covers.

To find old and rare prints, look through antiquing magazines for notices of specialty fairs. There, you'll find dealers from all over the country, and you'll be able to explore the full range of print subject matter, get detailed answers to any questions, and perhaps even start—or complete—a collection in a particular area.

Other Paper Art

Most people who love prints also can't resist paper collectibles. This is a broad category that embraces everything from old advertising trade cards, broadsides, paper dolls, timetables, playing cards, greeting cards, and vintage labels to letters or other documents from the past written with a fine flourish of handwriting.

Some collectors specialize in late 19th-century calligraphy exercises, which were a

It must have taken many patient hours for the creator of this cigar band "quilt" to piece together the fabric in such striking log cabin geometry, perhaps a gift for a husband or brother.

What better way to show it off than in an incised tramp art frame, another precise and exacting handicraft. Note how the deep colored mat enriches the colors of the cloth.

way of improving students' penmanship. With quill pens, students drew stylized lions, birds, and other creatures copied from instruction books. The pen strokes used for the pictures were practice for the same strokes used for letters. Today, these paper treasures look beautiful decorating the walls of antique-filled rooms.

As part of the backlash against the Industrial Revolution, at the turn of the 19th century, crafters resolved to create their own homemade treasures to decorate their rooms instead of buying mass-produced goods. Today, examples still survive; for instance, pictures pieced together completely from stamps, or collages of colored papers glued together to form a picture. Another popular craft of the day was cutwork, or "papyrotamia," the art of cutting detailed scenes—whether of people, flowers, or animals—and mounting them on contrasting colored papers. Some were as elaborate as the most intricate lacework.

Old wallpapers also fall into the category of paper art. Many, woodblock printed or handpainted in elaborate designs, are so beautiful they deserve to be displayed.

Paper collectors also seek out silhouettes, which were a way of recording a person's likeness before the advent of photography. They could be head profiles, full-length portraits, or even group portraits. Though many of the silhouette artists are anonymous, famous makers include Charles Willson Peale and Auguste Edouart, both of whom signed their art.

Old Photographs

Many people want to preserve heirloom family photographs, often displaying them en masse in hallways and family rooms. Rather than take chances with treasured originals, take the photographs to a commercial lab and make duplicates for framing. Keep the originals in an acid-free box (with the exception of albumen prints; see Conservation, page 32).

Most photo finishing shops are either equipped to make copies of vintage photos or will have an outside resource. They copy the image by scanning it into the computer. Scanning software applications allow one to scan either color or black and white, negatives or transparencies, into a digital format. For photos that need touch-ups, the restorer can then manipulate the image with software. Crackled, stained, or faded features can be erased, and, depending on the image, some lost portions can even be restored. Your

Wonderful old portraits from the past catch the eye with particular resonance when they are displayed with care. This baby picture is not only tripled matted, but outlined with a band of green ribbon. The mat on the engraving to its right is adorned with marbleized French tape.

pictures can also be altered: For instance, distracting photographer's seals can be removed, backgrounds changed, or a person can even be stripped out of a picture—and into another. This is known as imaging recomposition. The subtle hues of old hand-colored sepia photographs can be sensitively restored, and black and white photos can be colorized. Even the size can be changed to most anything you specify, although generally no larger than 8 by 10 inches.

The resulting photo is technically known as a dye sublimation output, an image on photographic stock. Once an image is saved in digital format, you can take the computer file on disk to a photo-imaging shop where it can be turned into a negative, allowing you to make prints.

If you don't have any heirloom photos to call your own, take the instant ancestors approach. The next time you visit your favorite antique shop, comb through the boxes filled with snapshots to find character-filled images that, depending on the subject matter, can provide a thought-provoking or humorous touch in a room when framed.

At flea markets, sift through boxes for panoramic photos—usually landscapes or group portraits—a wonderful way to decorate a narrow horizontal space over a doorway.

When displaying photos, do not use nonglare or nonreflective glass. Though it refracts light in such a way that it eliminates reflections, it also distorts the image.

Textiles

Delicate fabric and clothing—perhaps bits of tattered antique lace, a christening dress, needlepoint, or a pair of vintage gloves covered with intricate beadwork—that you've cherished for years but don't quite know how to show off can find happy lives under glass. Open your linen closet and bring that spectacular piece of fabric to light, whether it is a length of antique toile de Jouy or a splashy thirties print with an American West motif. So, too, an old scrap of a rag rug can pique interest when it is displayed in a frame.

Old textiles such as quilts and needlework samplers almost always show some signs of wear and tear. If you are thinking of having a piece repaired before you frame it, first consider whether it is precious to you for sentimental reasons, or for its historical significance. You might have a 19th-century sampler with

A framed Centennial banner and an unframed "jack" (a flag flown from a ship usually to indicate nationality) are just part of one homeowner's extensive flag collection—another artifact from the collection can be glimpsed through the doorway.

intricate stitchery made by your great-great-great aunt that is a fine example of its form, or the flag your grandfather once flew off the porch at his summer house—dear to your heart, but probably without any greater value. In these cases, if the piece is damaged in some way, have it repaired by a professional so that you can display it with deserved pride.

On the other hand, if the flag is an important historical artifact, then head to the local historical society, an antiques dealer who specializes in textiles or needlework, or a fabric conservator (see Resources, page 108) to assess its worth—do not alter it in any way before determining this. Some repairs actually decrease the value of a textile. A fabric conservator will be able to determine fabric content—whether something is cotton, a cotton-linen blend, or early rayon, all of which look and feel similar but require different cleaning and mending approaches—and how best to repair it.

For a less valuable textile, if it's musty or mildewed, air it out for a few weeks. If it's dust or dirt covered, place a stocking over your vacuum cleaner, put it on the lowest setting, and gently remove the surface debris. The less you do to your textile, the better.

Never use adhesive to mount textiles. Instead, sew them on. Measure your textile and have backing board or foam core cut to size. Attach the piece by folding the material over the board and securing it around the back by lacing in zigzags, lengthwise and widthwise.

If you are framing material that cannot or should not be folded over the sides of a backing board, such as a fragile lace collar or a christening dress, show it off whole. Make a slipcover for the board out of prewashed muslin or cotton, laced in the back. Then, with cotton thread, sew the material to the muslin using very tiny applique stitches. If the fabric scrap is fairly heavy, like a crocheted cotton doily or a carpet fragment, you'll need to sew it directly through the two fabric layers onto the board using a tapestry needle. Add a mat if you wish as a finishing touch.

Of course, you might want to frame your own contemporary needlework, maybe a sampler or crewelwork. In that case, many needlepoint shops will wash and block your work for you, or tell you how to do so, to prepare it for final framing.

Natural Objects

Objects picked up on a stroll along the beach or a walk through the woods are candidates

Sometimes, a collection becomes not what is inside a frame, but a part of the frame itself. Encrusted with a wealth of findings from the family button box, this special frame doesn't need to contain an image to engage the eye.

for framing, whether feathers, seashells, sand dollars, or starfish. Pressed flowers and leaves are also simple yet beautiful subjects.

While shells and feathers are ready-made for framing with hot glue, flowers, ferns, and leaves need special preparation. Collect in mid-morning, after the dew has evaporated from the petals and foliage. Spraying leaves or ferns with a coat of artists' clear acrylic spray before pressing will help to preserve their color. Place the botanicals between sheets of waxed paper, then press each item between the pages of a phone book or big encyclopedia. Put a heavy weight on top of that—another book or a brick—and leave for at least two weeks before peeking to see if it's dry.

Marigolds, mints, morning glories, pansies, Queen Anne's lace, daisies, and other relatively flat flowers all make fitting subjects, and can easily be framed by first arranging them on a mat board and then attaching them with glue or a hot glue gun.

Though organic objects such as these are bound to deteriorate over time, preserve them for as long as possible by displaying them away from a light source and sealed from air. Before framing, you could spray a starfish or seahorse

Splicing art with craft, the painter of this triple-pose pet portrait also fashioned the frame: a surround of glued-on dog biscuits in light and dark shades, varnished for longevity.

with varnish—in a well ventilated room, or better yet outdoors—to seal it and prolong its life under glass. Until you are ready to use them in a project, natural, organic objects should be stored in large boxes, wrapped in tissue with a neutral pH or prewashed muslin.

Conservation

Years ago, conservation of prints and other fragile media was a concern mainly among gallery owners and museum curators. Now, there is a more widespread awareness of the need to protect art from the dangers of acidity, heat, and light, and, fortunately, you will find that frame shops are well stocked with materials created expressly for protecting your treasures. While acid-free supplies are more costly, one only has to think of how quickly a newspaper, which is not acid-free, yellows and disintegrates, to understand the importance of using acid-free materials.

Whether you are working with a professional framer or doing it yourself, ensure that both the mat boards and backing are acid-free—which means they have a pH level of 7 or above. Acid content will result in degradation of photographic and other paper-based images, so also be sure your prints and photographs are stored in acid-free tissues, folders, and boxes. If you are already in possession of a framed print whose mat you'd rather keep, simply install an acid-free mat cut to size between the mat and the print.

In addition to acid-free mat board, be sure to use a sealing method that uses archival-quality board or backing paper. Key words to look for when buying such materials are conservation quality, museum quality, or archival quality, all of which mean that they are chemically stable and acid-free. When choosing mat board, look for the words rag or alphacellulose mat (known in the trade as alpha mat); ordinary board is made from wood pulp, which contains lignin, a substance that will decay and so is dangerous to have around anything that's paper based.

Of course, to every rule there is an exception, and this one is albumen prints, 19th-century photographs that used eggwhites as a gel medium. These photographs actually need a slightly acidic environment, so display them on unbuffered rag board (the buffering agent is calcium carbonate) and store them in unbuffered rag boxes. Consult an expert if you need to know how to handle albumen prints.

Never store or display art of value or heirloom quality (including original photos) in rooms subject to wide variations in temperature and humidity, such as a bathroom or kitchen. Use common sense: You wouldn't want harm to come to your father's watercolors, but you might relax a bit about a thrift shop photo that merely serves a decorative purpose. A humid environment also encourages insects, which are harmful to organic materials like paper.

Always keep paper artwork stored flat, not rolled. Strong light is also anathema—it fades and dries—so position your heirloom or valuable paper artwork and photos out of direct sunlight. If you have very valuable artwork, consider using ultraviolet-proof Plexiglas (also known as conservation or museum-grade glass) or a UV filter on your windows and opting for incandescent over fluorescent light. Fluorescent light, like sunlight, contains high levels of ultraviolet radiation, which undermines the chemical bond in organic materials such as paper. Incandescent light emits comparatively miniscule amounts of ultraviolet radiation.

Art of any kind should never be placed close to a heat source, such as a radiator, fireplace, or air duct. Not only are the changes of temperature detrimental to any surface, but soot and grime can harm the work.

Even if artwork is displayed away from heat and light, it can still be affected by pollutants if there is a gap in the frame that exposes it to air. So if you have inexpensive sandwich frames of glass and mat board clipped together, seal the join with acid-free linen or paper tape to prevent dust, pollen, and other pollutants from slipping in.

Should a fine old print be damaged, never try to clean or restore it yourself. Instead, take it to a paper conservator. Since the print is liable to be on a mix of handmade papers, only a professional can determine how to repair such a varied composition.

Finally, always use both hands to pick up a matted or unmatted piece of paper. When cleaning pictures under glass, do not spray cleaning fluid directly on the glass, as it may seep underneath. Instead, wipe it with a slightly dampened cloth.

Textiles have the same sort of conservation considerations as paper art. The things that are the enemies of paper—humidity, dirt, sunlight, and insects—attack fabric as well. Some collectors rotate their textiles on display to minimize exposure to sunlight. They also take the added precaution of not using cleaners containing bleach, ammonia, or chlorine in the vicinity of valuable fabric, as the chemicals can become airborne and harm it.

As with paper, use acid-free materials to show off your fabrics—acid-free foam core is the material of choice for a base, though you could use mat board with lighter textiles.

In the end, all of the care you take with your textiles, paintings, photographs, and other paper-based artwork will ensure that your collections will become an heirloom for future generations.

chapter two

the art of framing

Let the object of your desire be your guide to the perfect frame. Depending on the subject, the ideal frame might be a richly carved gilt surround or a minimalist design of two pieces of glass sandwiched together. Matching frames, mats, and subjects is an art rooted in history and swayed by fashion. From the 15th- and 16th-century Dutch painters, who would allow colors and details of their paintings, such as robes, to spill out onto the frame, to Impressionists Georges Seurat and Vincent van Gogh, who actually painted borders as part of their paintings to enhance the effects of the picture, artists have long had a passionate interest in just how their works are displayed.

But over the years wealthy patrons and collectors have reframed pictures to suit their tastes—or simply to match their decor. Today we usually try to pair a frame with the period or mood of the subject. An American primitive painting, for example, would call for an equally simple wood frame. However, we have also expanded the definition of what constitutes a frame and turned our attention to frames as works of art in themselves, while not losing sight of their original role as a means of defining and enhancing the art.

In this chapter, you'll find 13 step-by-step projects that are perfect unions of frames, mats, and subjects, and are designed to inspire your framing. The possibilities range from transforming a ready-made picture frame with copper foil or a covering of fabric to constructing your own from chipboard and gift wrap.

When it comes to trying your hand at framing with traditional moldings and mats, however, it is advisable to take a class (or at least find a mentor!) to find out just how it's done. Traditional framing involves expenditures on such things as mat cutters, so it's up to you to determine whether to attempt it at home or to take your frameables to a professional, who offers not only materials and services but years of expertise.

About Frames

Anyone who has ever stepped into a frame shop knows that there is an enormous variety of frame styles available (and an equally large framing vocabulary). Yet frames didn't start off that way: In medieval times, they were originally part of the artwork itself, usually meant to be displayed as altarpieces. In that sense, the first frames were really "shrines" for the artwork within. It wasn't until the 16th century that frames as we know them became detachable objects.

Frames continue to evolve today—they could be almost anything you'd like them to be. But as with any subject, you need to know the basics before you can improvise. To begin, the language of framing is useful to know when you're out antiquing, at a gallery, or paying a visit to the crafts shop or the framer.

The sides of a frame, called the molding, are the most noticeable aspect of a frame. With mass-produced frames, the joints of the molding are visible. The joints of a handmade frame, by contrast, are less pronounced—even invisible—since the finish is applied after it is joined.

There are three basic frame profiles—that is, the shape of the molding:

■ The spoon frame (also called the hollow, cove, or swept frame) slopes into the picture, drawing the eye inward.

■ Reverse frames slant away from the picture and slope toward the wall, creating a bridge between frame and background. Such a frame can be concave (also known as reverse hollow) or convex (also called bolection). With such

Prints of architectural details almost touch the dentil moldings in this high-ceilinged room. A simple treatment of white mats and skinny metal frames emphasizes the prints' geometry, while a strong central image anchors the arrangement.

frames, the sight edge—the edge nearest the painting—is more pronounced.

■ Flatfaced, or level, frames are simply that: They are composed of straight planes, connected at 90-degree angles.

Of course, within these profiles, there are gentle slopes and more pronounced ones. But all traditional moldings fit into these basic categories. Regardless of its profile, a frame can be made of any number of materials.

The most inexpensive and versatile is the aluminum frame, available in many colors and finishes, including classic black, white, gold, and silver. When in doubt, the combination of a basic black metal frame with a white mat is foolproof. It not only gives definition to black and white photos, but works well with posters. Aluminum frames in any color, sensitively paired with the right colored mats, are also good choices for children's artwork.

Wood frames are equally common, but a bit more expensive. They can be treated (limed or stained), ornate or simple, dark or light. Early American frames are perhaps the simplest of all: plain, flat moldings of black painted pine, or native woods, such as maple or fruitwoods, left completely natural.

Wood tends to be a good choice for a country look and is the perfect complement to paintings with primitive subjects or to pastoral flower art. The exception, of course, is gilt wood frames, which give a more formal feeling and can call for grander subjects, such as posed portraits.

Wood frames can also be decorated with special effects such as sponging, faux tortoise-shell, stenciling, and japanning. These techniques offer an opportunity to spruce up old and forgotten frames and add instant cheer or drama to a room for very little money. You might paint a frame and pick up the dominant colors of the subject, or stencil a tiny fruit motif on a frame destined to show off a print of apples in a bowl, for example.

Thanks to contemporary production methods, there are also many wood frames available with laminate treatments that resemble hand-done techniques like marbleizing, and natural wood features such as burling or bamboo.

Frame shops also offer silver-leaf frames. Unlike gold, they provide a cool counterpoint to a painting. If a painting has hot, tropical colors, silver adds a note of relief. On the other hand, if a picture has touches of soft pinks and grays, silver acts in soothing harmony.

Silver or silverplate frames are wonderful for photographs. As mentioned before, ordinary aluminum flat frames also have silver finishes; they are a lightweight alternative to silver or silver-leaf frames, but they are completely unembellished.

framing terms

acid-free having a pH level of 7 or above

archival quality materials that are chemically stable, that is, acid-free; also known as museum or conservation quality

backboard mat board on which an image is fixed

beveled edge angled edge of a mat window

bolection a convex reverse frame

close framing framing without a mat

conservation quality see archival quality

cove frame see spoon frame

double mat mat with two front boards

fillet inner frame that forms a bridge between painting and frame, often painted or gilt

flatfaced frame frame with flat profile, turning at 90-degree angles; also known as a level frame

floating mounting an image on top of a mat so its edges show

french mat general term for a hand-washed mat (e.g., one with washlines) or one with gold foil decoration

french tape decorative sheets to cut into strips and apply to a mat

front board the front mat board, which contains the window for displaying art; also known as a window board or blank

hollow frame see spoon frame

molding raw or ready-made sections cut to size to make a frame

museum quality see archival quality

profile shape of a frame's molding

rabbet groove in which the mat or artwork sits in the inside edge of the frame; the rabbet must be large enough to accommodate the thickness of the picture or fabric

reverse frame frame that angles away from a picture toward the wall

reverse hollow a concave reverse frame

spacer inner piece of clear plastic or wood molding that separates the glass from the artwork

spoon frame frame that slopes into the picture, drawing the eye inward; also known as a hollow, cove, or swept frame

swept frame see spoon frame

washline application of lines of watercolor or gouache paint to follow the outline of a window mat opening; can be combined with pen and ink

weighting cutting the mat bottom wider to compensate for the eye's natural tendency to see the bottom as smaller than the other three sides

Clear glass is also an option. A floating glass frame—two pieces of glass sandwiched together—not only makes a good frame for natural objects such as pressed leaves and flowers, where you want to play up the delicacy of the subject, but also works well with paper items that you would like to view from both sides, such as postcards or opera bills.

The increasing availability of shadow boxes is a boon to collectors, because they are designed to display three-dimensional objects. You can buy a ready-made shadow box frame (some equipped with dividers or compartments), design and build your own, or enlist the services of a professional framer. A small curio or postman's cabinet—with multiple cubbyholes—also makes a good shadow box frame. Reproductions are available through catalogs. Indeed, almost any box-shaped object—an old shuttered desk drawer or shuttered cabinet—can be converted to a shadow box. Such frames needn't sit upright: They can be placed flat on tables to be admired.

Objects are mounted in shadow boxes in different ways from traditional framing. With a foamboard backing covered with pretty paper, fabric, or artist's canvas, you can use a needle and thread to secure your lightweight treasures. Heavier items require either a hot glue gun, heavy duty adhesive, or fishing line.

Folk frames, which can be antique or new, are another important category. Made from anything that an artist sees fit to use—seashells, leather, buttons, silverware, tools—these frames are art in themselves, involving specialized techniques such as whittling or puzzle construction. Some collectors let them stand on their own without art inside. Folk frames can defy the traditional wisdom about frames—that they are intended to enhance the art and to function almost at a subliminal level without distracting the viewer's attention. Many folk frames, such as tramp art frames, become part of the art itself.

When pairing a folk frame with a picture, try to imagine its origins and the personality of the creator. For instance, an 1880's shadow box frame embellished with strips of leather decoration might be the perfect vehicle for antique hunting equipment.

Though it's certainly a good rule of thumb to seek out a frame that matches a picture's period, there is room for interpretation. After all, a frame that exactly replicates the spirit of a painting can look contrived. So long as a frame is connected to a picture by color,

In this collection of perfectly preserved sheet music dating back to World War I, variations in frame treatment add another level of visual interest. Like a harmonious pattern of notes, red and black frames alternate rhythmically around the even-numbered grouping. Mats are equally varied: dark, pale, or none at all.

texture, or mood, it can be a good match. Rules are meant to be broken. Most contemporary art calls for simpler frames—generally speaking. But a contemporary work can look absolutely wonderful in an antique frame— perhaps an abstract drawing married to a baroque wood frame that captures the restless quality of the picture itself. At the same time, a 19th-century oil painting covered in layers of lacquer, as was the Victorian custom, can have such a brooding presence that a contemporary silver-finish metal frame might be just the right light-catching counterpoint.

As a final consideration, don't feel bound to match the size of the frame exactly with that of the picture. Generally, the proportions of the frame should reflect the proportions of the art. But the size of the frame can vary. For example, a larger frame will always attract more attention to a smaller work of art. In fact, most people automatically choose a frame with a width that is too narrow for the art—so try to go a few sizes larger than your first choice.

About Mats

On its most practical level, the mat prevents a picture or photo from making direct contact with the frame and therefore being damaged by condensation. However, a mat also serves an aesthetic purpose, enhancing certain colors in a print, for instance, or creating the illusion of a different image size, depending on how the mat is cut. Its width can be cut to any size, from a sliver glimpsed under another mat to a broad band as much as a foot across. A mat's thickness can range anywhere from two- to twelve-ply; four-ply ($1/16$ inch) is standard.

The next time you visit a gallery, take note of how the artwork is matted. Chances are, the bottom border of the mat will be at least a half inch wider than the other three sides. This treatment, known as weighting, compensates for the fact that your eye will automatically perceive the bottom portion as being narrower than the other three sides. The extra measurement cancels out this optical illusion. Were it not done, the picture would seem to be sinking down in the frame.

You might notice as well that the mats used by the gallery are more sizable than the norm. A larger mat tends to give artwork more importance and a sense of balance. If the mat is too small, the picture looks squeezed in by the frame. Keep in mind that a mat's thickness also affects your perception—the deeper the mat, the more your eye is drawn to the art within. Some framers favor double mats—that is, using two mats with different window sizes, often in contrasting colors, to create a sense of perspective.

While most often pictures are framed

under a mat, sometimes they are "floated" on top of the top mat. This is done to show off interesting or timeworn edges of paper ephemera or to highlight the irregular contours of the medium on which an artwork is created. Another unusual yet easy-to-achieve effect comes from using French tape, a decorative material available in sheets, which can be cut into strips of varying widths and attached to the mat. Available in a variety of patterns and colors and most variations of marbleizing, the tape can add a rich band of color to an otherwise austere framed and matted picture.

Framed Effects

There are no hard-and-fast rules for matching a frame with a piece of art, but here are a few guidelines:

■ With paintings that rely on perspective, such as landscape paintings and portraits with background details, use a spoon frame that slopes inward and therefore draws your eye into the picture.

■ Flower paintings and still lifes suit reverse profile frames, which angle away from the image and connect it with its surroundings.

■ Choose flat, unadorned frames for modern works whose compelling styles require minimal adornment. Plain or pickled wood is often a good choice.

■ If your collection comprises sporting, equestrian, or other masculine themes, consider the classic choice: a veneered or dark wood frame.

■ Black painted frames make colors more vibrant; with a narrow fillet of gold, the effect is positively sparkling.

■ Oval frames or frames with rounded corners work well with watercolors or portraits (painted or photographed) that include both heads and shoulders.

■ A light touch of gold or silver in the frame suits watercolors, while old photos, silhouettes, and portraits benefit from a dark wood surround.

Mat Matches

While shades of classic white are almost always a good choice for mats, a world of possibilities awaits those willing to experiment:

■ Antique prints and watercolors look charming with fine French hand-washed mats in dusty colors, perhaps hand-milled with gold foil. This 18th-century tradition is still beautiful today. Other decorative mats include those embellished with a painted line, referred to as a washline border or watercolor wash border.

■ When choosing a mat for photographs, use a bright white shade for new photographs and an antique white shade for older ones. Don't mat old black and white family photos with a mat that is brighter than the tones of the picture, which can make the photographs seem drab. A touch of silver or gold along the mat bevel will give the print a reflective quality.

■ Special effects, such as using a mat flecked with gold, can add impact to a picture—and sometimes make an ordinary print look more appealing. Of course, you can decorate mats too: Spattering, stippling, sponging, marbleizing, or covering in fabric are just a few techniques that work well.

■ With their wealth of detail, cartoons tend to benefit from pale, broad, unobtrusive mats paired with plain black frames.

■ If your print is foxed (discolored) or marred in some way, use a colored mat to distract the eye.

■ When matting old prints, consider using a two-toned double mat: a pale inner mat, perhaps ornamented with a washline, contained within a slightly darker outer mat.

■ Architectural prints and maps look wonderful matted with deep colored mats in rich 19th-century colors like India red, Havana brown, and bottle green.

■ Think of gold as a neutral, and use it with any work of art you like—not just with its traditional match, oil paintings. Gold provides a sense of warmth and calm, while actually reflecting light onto the work.

■ Group family pictures together in a multi-windowed mat.

■ If you are unsure about which colored mat looks best with your art, pair your artwork with different paint chips or even selections from a box of crayons to see which color suits it best. This way, you won't be called upon to make a spur-of-the-moment decision at the frame shop.

■ Try to look at mats in the light and against the wall where they will be placed.

■ When choosing a colored mat, pick up a secondary color, if possible, in the picture or document. If you echo the primary color in the mat, the effect could be overwhelming. Just as with any home decorating question, consult the color wheel for complementary and analogous combinations.

■ Classic gray and black mats add drama to gold frames.

■ Bold colored mats are wonderful with whimsical frameables, such as playing cards or your grade school report card.

■ Don't make the mat the same width as the frame: for instance, 2-inch mat, 2-inch frame. The effect is dull and predictable.

When a frame is so spectacular that no image suits it, a mirror is a good option. This mirror, in an urban living room, doesn't compete with its ornate frame. The two paintings that hang alongside complement the larger frame's gold finish, yet a touch of red in their moldings visually unites them with the oxblood walls.

decoupage
frame

Decoupage is a craft you've probably been practicing since childhood. Like the cut and paste of grade school, it's as simple as cutting paper, pasting it on a frame and then covering with varnish. When choosing paper for a decoupage frame, think about the artwork to be framed. Here, we used old sheet music from a second-hand store because the man pictured especially loved music. But don't limit yourself to old or rare paper; sources for paper can be as varied as candy wrappers, magazines, catalogs, stamps, Christmas cards, wallpaper scraps, gift wrap, and maps.

1. Remove the backing materials and glass from the frame. Lightly sand the frame and brush off the dust. If you're not planning on covering the whole frame with decoupage, stain the front and sides of the frame and allow to dry.

2. With the scissors, cut the paper into strips or carefully cut around the images on the paper you want to use. Arrange the paper on the frame in a decorative pattern, holding the paper down with the tape and trying different patterns until you find a design you like. One by one, remove the papers from the frame, discard the tape, and with a brush, apply a light coat of paste to the back. Place the paper back on the frame and clean off any excess paste with dampened cotton balls.

3. With a brush, apply 2 or 3 coats of varnish, allowing it to dry between coats. Insert the glass, mat, artwork, and backing to complete the frame.

MATERIALS

flatfaced unfinished wooden frame

water-based stain (optional)

old sheet music or other interesting paper

satin or matte water-based varnish

TOOLS

fine sandpaper

small sharp scissors

removable tape, such as 3M's Scotch Brand Removable Tape

foam brushes

YES! brand all purpose paste or wallpaper paste

cotton balls

If bubbles appear in the paper while drying, simply poke them with a pin and smooth out the paper. You might also consider leaving minor bubbles in the finished frame to enhance the aged, worn appearance.

❖   ❖   ❖

aged decoupage
frame

Decoupage accents of vintage paper covered with elegant handwriting (found in an antique shop) create this heirloom-style frame perfect for framing old, sepia-toned photos. Here the frame has been stained to enhance the aged effect while the four-panel design with corner squares complements the reverse molding frame. To preserve original papers, use color copies, but talk to your copy shop representative beforehand: Many copiers cannot reproduce the sepia tone of aged paper well.

1. Remove the backing materials and glass from the frame. Lightly sand the frame and brush off the dust. Stain the inner and outer edges of the frame and allow to dry.

2. On the cutting mat with the X-Acto knife and a ruler, carefully cut the papers into strips and squares according to the dimensions of the frame and the design. With a foam brush, apply a light, smooth coat of paste to the back of one piece of paper and place on the frame. With a cotton ball, smooth the paper down and clean off any excess paste. Continue with the remaining strips of paper until the design is complete. Allow to dry overnight.

3. Soak a cotton ball in the tea. Squeeze lightly, then run it along the outside edge of the glued paper, creating an even, aged look around the perimeter. Allow to dry.

4. With a foam brush apply 3 coats of varnish, allowing it to dry between coats. Insert the glass, mat, artwork, and backing to complete the frame.

❖   ❖   ❖

MATERIALS

reverse molding unfinished wooden frame

antique pine water-based stain

vintage handwritten papers

strong-brewed tea, room temperature

satin water-based varnish

TOOLS

fine sandpaper

cutting board or cardboard

X-Acto knife

foam brushes

YES! brand all-purpose paste or wallpaper paste

cotton balls

corrugated cardboard
shadow box frame

The natural simplicity of corrugated cardboard lends itself well to this small shadow box—perfect for starfish, pine cones, or other objects found outdoors.

1. On the cutting mat with a ruler, the triangle, and X-Acto knife, cut a 4- by 6-inch rectangle from the cardboard. Using it as a template, cut 7 more pieces with the corrugation all going in the same direction. Cut one more 4- by 6-inch rectangle of cardboard, but with the corrugation going in the opposite direction; set aside—this will be the backing piece.

2. Cut out a 2- by 4-inch window from one piece of cardboard, leaving a 1-inch-wide frame. Using this piece as a template, trace the window with a pencil on each of the cardboard rectangles (except for the backing piece); cut away the inside pieces.

3. On the back of one of the frame pieces, draw a rectangle $3/8$ inch in from the outside edges. Mark 2 dots $3/8$ inch in from each corner of the rectangle. With the hole punch, create 8 holes for the raffia ties.

4. Hold this piece up to the smooth side of each framing piece and mark the hole placement with a pencil. Then, punch holes through each piece, including the backing piece.

5. With the corrugation face up, stack all of the pieces with the backing piece at the back, lining up the holes. Thread a few short strips of raffia through the holes of each bottom corner and tie in the front. Thread longer strips of raffia through the top left, then through the top right holes. Tie the ends together to make a loop for hanging.

6. Glue the object to be framed on the backing piece.

❖   ❖   ❖

MATERIALS

large sheet of natural colored corrugated cardboard, at least 22 x 14 inches

raffia

TOOLS

cutting mat or cardboard

triangle

X-Acto knife

small hole punch

craft glue

burnished copper frame

Liver of sulfur, a pungent-smelling yellow liquid available at art supply stores in four-ounce bottles, is commonly used by metalsmiths and artisans to age and darken copper. Immersing the metal completely will quickly produce a black finish, but when applied with restraint, liver of sulfur can create wonderful patterns in purple, gray, and blue-black—colors that can then be enhanced or altered by polishing the dry surface with steel wool.

1. Remove the backing materials and glass from the frame. Wear protective gloves when working with foil. Lay the copper foil on a flat work surface and place the frame face down on top. With the frame as a guide, use a pen to mark a rectangle 2 inches larger all around on the foil. Cut out the rectangle with scissors.

2. Place the foil rectangle on the cutting mat and position the frame in the center. With a pen, draw diagonal lines from opposite corners of the frame window to create an "X." Remove the frame. With the X-Acto knife and ruler, cut along the marked X. Cut away most of the triangular sections, leaving enough foil to bend around the lip and rabbet of the window. Save the scraps for testing coloring techniques. With the paint brush, coat the interior edges of the wood frame at the corners with copper-colored acrylic paint. Let dry.

3. Move the foil piece and scraps to a newspaper-covered work area. With cotton balls and alcohol, clean the surface of the copper thoroughly, removing all fingerprints and oil. Dilute 1 teaspoon liver of sulfur in 4 cups water. Wearing rubber gloves, dip a cotton ball into the solution and dab or run the cotton along the surface of a scrap piece of copper. Watch as the coloration develops as you continue to add the solution. The metal will continue to darken as the copper dries.

MATERIALS

flatfaced unfinished hardwood frame

36-gauge copper foil

copper-colored acrylic paint

liver of sulfur

TOOLS

protective work gloves

metal-edged ruler

X-Acto knife

cutting mat or cardboard

small paint brush

cotton balls

alcohol

rubber gloves

steel wool

heavy-duty spray adhesive

burnishing tool

Butcher's wax

The frames in the picture on page 54 show 2 basic painting techniques. The top features an organic pattern created by blotting and dabbing the solution over some areas of the surface in an irregular fashion, leaving some of the copper as it is. The other style was created by dragging the solution over the surface with a cotton ball in long horizontal strokes, creating a striated pattern. After finding a technique you are happy with, color the frame piece. Allow the foil to dry completely. If desired, repeat to darken the copper further.

4. Once the copper is dry and you are satisfied with its color, use steel wool to create a brushed look on the surface. Rub the steel wool in a circular or vertical fashion, depending on the finish desired. Experiment with your scrap pieces to test the finishing technique.

5. Lay the foil face down on a newspaper-covered work surface. Spray adhesive on the back. Hold the frame face down over the foil, making sure the window is centered, and press the frame into place. Turn the frame over and press the foil onto the front of the frame, from the window out to the edges. With a burnishing tool, bend the foil onto and around the window lip and rabbet.

6. Place the frame face down and with a pen, mark the approximate 2-by 2-inch squares at each outside corner of the copper. With the X-Acto knife, cut out the corners. Adhere the foil to the frame's edges and back: Using your fingers, bend the foil around one edge at a time, burnishing each edge from front to back. Miter the back corner pieces by trimming the overlapping foil diagonally.

7. With a soft cloth, polish the entire surface of the copper frame with Butcher's wax to protect the patina. Insert the glass, mat, artwork, and backing to complete the frame.

❖　❖　❖

The glow of a burnished frame—copper or, opposite, gold—is very popular, although care should be taken not to let candles damage artwork.

distressed wood frame

Water-based color stains have many benefits—not only do they clean up with just soap and water, but they can be applied and wiped off like regular stains to show wood grain or they can be applied thickly and opaquely like paint (as we have done here). This technique for two-tone distressing creates a stronger color contrast between the stains than would happen by merely sanding through layers of color. The fabric-covered foam core mat provides an ideal background for three-dimensional objects such as this child's mitten, which is simply tacked onto the foam core with small pins. We left the glass out of the frame for a heightened textural feeling, but you may want to include it if the item you are framing is flatter. If so, use chipboard, instead of foam core, for the mat.

1. Remove the backing materials and glass from the frame. Lightly sand the frame and brush off the dust. With a foam brush, apply 2 liberal coats of the cranberry stain, using the brush to even out the appearance. Allow the frame to dry between coats. It should have a dull, solid, paint-like finish.

2. Apply 2 coats of green stain, also liberally and evenly with a foam brush, but leave the edges of the frame bare to create a slightly uneven line and to let the cranberry stain show through, again allowing the frame to dry between coats.

3. Lightly sand the frame to distress the finish where additional weathering is desired. With a foam brush, apply 2 coats of varnish, letting it dry between coats.

4. To make the mat: On the cutting mat, cut a piece from the foam core with the X-Acto knife to the size that will fit in the rabbet of the frame. If you plan to include the glass in the frame, use chipboard.

MATERIALS

flatfaced wooden frame

cranberry-colored water-based stain

deep green water-based stain

satin water-based varnish

1/8-inch foam core or 2-ply chipboard

fabric to cover the mat

TOOLS

fine sandpaper

foam brushes

cutting mat or cardboard

X-Acto knife

spray adhesive appropriate to bond fabrics to paper, such as Spra-Ment Craft & Display Adhesive from 3M

5. Lay the fabric for the mat face down and press with an iron to remove any wrinkles. Cut out a rectangle that is $1/2$ to 2 inches larger than the mat on all sides. Move the fabric to a newspaper-covered work area. Keeping the fabric as smooth as possible, spray adhesive on the wrong side of the fabric. Place the mat in the center of the fabric, and press gently to seal the fabric to the mat. Fold the corners of the fabric diagonally over the edges of the mat, and press to adhere. Then, fold the sides of the fabric around to the back of the mat, making sure that the fabric lies smoothly and is firmly glued in place.

6. If not using the glass, attach the object to be framed to the foam core mat with small pins or tacks and then insert the fabric-covered mat and backing materials into the frame. If using the glass, simply insert the glass, object to be framed, chipboard mat, and backing materials to complete the frame.

❖   ❖   ❖

A three-dimensional effect is achieved here by a window "framed" with a mix of glued-on seashells and starfish. Shadow box specimens from a Paris flea market flank the window, and on the table below, Victorian shellboxes anchor this natural history collection.

silver-lipped frame

This unique frame is contemporary, yet reminiscent of the studded trunks and valises of our grandparents. Simply cut, fold, and tack strips of thick aluminum foil (available at craft stores) to the edges or surfaces of an existing frame. The silver border can highlight a cherished photo or add interest to a special newspaper clipping or announcement. Choose small nails that do not exceed the thickness of the frame and that will match the color of the foil or pick up the color of the wood stain.

1. Remove the backing materials and glass from the frame. Prepare the frame by lightly sanding the inside edge of the frame window. With the brush, apply silver paint or liquid leaf to the inner edge of the window. Allow the paint to dry.

2. Wear protective gloves when working with foil. Place a sheet of foil on the cutting mat. Lay the frame face down over the foil. With a pen, trace the inside edge of the frame onto the foil. Remove the frame from the foil.

3. With the ruler, measure and draw a rectangle 1 inch larger all around than the first rectangle. Draw another rectangle 1/2 inch inside of the first marked rectangle. With the ruler and X-Acto knife, cut along the outside rectangle. Carefully cut out and trim the foil inside the innermost rectangle. Make diagonal cuts from each corner of the inside rectangle to the corresponding corner of the middle rectangle.

4. Fold an 1/8-inch hem around the outside of the foil square using the ruler as a guide for bending the edges. Lay the hemmed foil over the frame, and gently bend each inner flap snugly around the lip of the frame.

MATERIALS

flatfaced wooden frame

silver paint or liquid leaf

36-gauge aluminum foil

TOOLS

fine sandpaper

small brush

protective work gloves

cutting mat or cardboard

metal-edged ruler

X-Acto knife

1mm x 13mm nails

fine steel wool

Butcher's wax

5. Lay the frame face up on a sturdy work surface. With firm, even strokes, tap nails around the hemmed edge of the foil, spacing the nails at $1/2$-inch intervals.

6. With the steel wool, brush the foil surface in a small circular pattern to add a matte sheen. (Slide pieces of paper under the edges of the foil to protect the wood while sanding.) To protect the metal, polish the surface with Butcher's wax applied with a soft cloth. Insert the glass, mat, artwork, and backing to complete the frame.

Metals, if not protected, will react with their environment. This produces their coloring or patina. If you want the metallic foil on your frames to continue to age and patinate, just skip the final polishing of Butcher's wax.

❖   ❖   ❖

Found materials make excellent frames, as shown in this kitchen where a favorite image has been carefully applied to an old kitchen tray.

paper-covered envelope frame

Perfect for a child's room, this quick and simple gift wrap envelope frame is bright with color and style. When choosing a paper, consider the placement of the design on the frame—it might be hard to read a large pattern on a small frame, for example—and adapt the size and width of the frame to best complement the image you're framing. You could also try this with handmade paper, the comics section of the Sunday paper, or even parchment stationery.

1. On the cutting mat with a ruler, the triangle and X-Acto knife, cut a 5- by 7-inch piece of chipboard to make the front piece. Mark a 3- by 5-inch window in the center and cut it out with the X-Acto knife. Cut a 5- by 6½-inch piece of chipboard for the backing.

2. Cut a 9- by 16-inch piece of gift wrap. Place the paper, wrong side up, on a newspaper-covered work area and spray with adhesive.

3. Place the front piece carefully on the paper, ¾ inch from one short side, and centered between the long sides. Fold the ¾-inch overhang back over onto the front piece. With a pencil, draw diagonal lines on the paper from opposite corners of the front window to create an "X." With the X-Acto knife and ruler, cut along the marked X. Fold one triangular flap up onto the back of the chipboard frame and press to adhere. Trim the point of the triangle if it extends beyond the frame edge. Repeat for each of the remaining flaps.

4. Place the backing piece onto the gift wrap just underneath the front piece, short end to short end, leaving about ⅛ inch between the pieces. Press to adhere it to the paper. There should be about 1 inch of paper at the bottom of the backing piece. Fold this over onto the

MATERIALS

2-ply chipboard at least 10- by 14-inches

gift wrap paper

TOOLS

triangle

X-Acto knife

spray adhesive

backing piece and press to seal. Then, fold the whole backing piece over the front piece, so the gift wrap on the sides meets, sticky side to sticky side. The backing piece should end $1/2$ inch shorter at the top than the frame piece; this is the opening that you'll use to insert the picture.

5. As if you were wrapping a gift, fold in the corners to make 2 flaps on each side. Carefully spray adhesive just on the flaps and fold the flaps over onto the back of the frame. Press to adhere. Insert the artwork in the opening at the top.

❖   ❖   ❖

Paper lends itself not only to making a frame but also to being framed. Here, a piece of framed vintage wallpaper echoes the pattern of the wall covering so closely—but not exactly—that your eye is drawn to look carefully at both.

distressed recycled wood frame

A found piece of wood can easily become the backing for a picture. This frame uses the top of an old step stool picked up at a yard sale. Take advantage of any interesting fixtures (like the hinges on this piece) you might have on hand to hang the frame. Have a glass or frame shop cut the glass for you and ask the glass cutter to sand the edges to eliminate sharp corners.

1. Clean the wood piece with the oil soap and let it dry. Sand with steel wool to remove dirt and any shedding paint chips. Continue to sand, wearing through various areas of paint to create a distressed finish. If the wood is new, you may want to create an aged look: Cover the front and sides of the wood with crackle medium followed by acrylic paint. Allow to dry. Rub out the finish with steel wool to distress the surface.

2. With the foam brush, apply 2 coats of varnish to the wood, following manufacturer's instructions. Allow to dry.

3. Center the artwork over the finished wood. With a ruler and pencil, lightly mark the position for the glass retainers, 1 to 2 inches in from each corner at the top and the bottom of the artwork. Lay the glass over the top of the artwork and test the positioning of the retainers so they sit comfortably just outside the glass.

4. Screw the stabilizing screws of the glass retainers into the wood. Insert the other screws into the holes until they rest firmly, but not tightly, against the glass.

5. Screw 2 hinges or eyehooks to the top outside edges of the wood. Measure and cut desired length of twine, allowing 2 inches for knotting. Thread the twine through a hole in each hinge or eyehook, securing each end with overhand knots.

❖   ❖   ❖

MATERIALS

piece of painted wood, at least $^5/_8$-inch-thick and approximately 2 inches larger all around than the artwork

acrylic crackle medium and acrylic paint (optional)

matte acrylic varnish

4 glasses retainers (available at specialty hardware stores)

piece of picture frame glass measuring the same size artwork

hinges, eye hooks, or other antique fixtures (if needed for hanging)

heavy jute twine

TOOLS

Murphy's Oil Soap

steel wool

foam brush

ribbon-wrapped glass frames

These frames are perfect for little mementoes, like the cancelled stamps, first fallen leaf of fall, and antique calling card shown here. But any little token, be it a miniature photograph or a ticket stub from a memorable concert, will be well displayed in these delicate, versatile frames. We show you two styles of frames here: a glass-to-glass "sandwich" floating frame and a glass and chipboard combination with a corrugated cardboard mat. Have a glass or frame shop cut the glass and sand the edges for you. You may want to use non-glare glass for frames with backing, but only clear glass is appropriate for floating frames.

1. With a dab or two of rubber cement, glue the reverse side of the object to one piece of glass or the cardboard. If using the cardboard backing, assemble the frame by placing the piece of glass in front and the piece of chipboard in back. If not using the cardboard, simply place the second piece of glass in front. Tie the pieces together with ribbon, twine, or raffia.

2. If you find that the tie is not strong enough to hold the 2 glass pieces firmly together, wrap the perimeter with foil tape.

Stained-glass foil tape, a metallic tape that comes in a variety of widths, is available from stained glass suppliers (look in the yellow pages under stained glass). Depending on the width, the tape can either fit just on the outside edges of the glass or can overlap the edges to create a narrow border.

MATERIALS

1 or 2 pieces 4- x 4-inch, $1/16$-inch-thick picture frame glass

4- x 4-inch piece corrugated cardboard (optional)

4- x 4-inch piece chipboard (optional)

ribbon, twine, or raffia

copper or silver stained-glass foil tape (optional)

TOOLS

rubber cement

❖　❖　❖

glass etched frame

Slightly frosting parts of the glass with etching cream is a nice way to personalize or spruce up a plain clip frame. We etched festive stars for this child's artwork, but you could also use stencil letters to etch the budding artist's name. You'll get the best results when etching by using large figures with straight or slightly curved edges rather than intricate designs, which may not leave a clean image. The frosted pattern appears best over dark mats. Etching cream is extremely caustic, so wear rubber gloves and goggles when using it.

1. Remove the clips from the glass and clean the glass well with glass cleaner. Fingerprints and dirt can leave a residue, which will make the final etched pattern less even.

2. Remove the backing from the contact paper and place the paper on one side of the glass. Transfer your design to the contact paper using the stencil and pencil, rubber stamp and ink, or by drawing freehand. If using a stamp, try to limit the amount of ink that is transferred to the vinyl, since it, too, can leave a residue on the glass.

3. With the X-Acto knife, carefully cut along the edges of the design. Remove the inside pieces defining the pattern. These will be the areas that will be etched.

4. Cover your index finger with a paper towel and run it along the cut edges, ensuring that there is an even, firm contact between the vinyl and glass. With a Q-tip and glass cleaner, lightly clean any areas of the glass that may have become dirty with ink or fingerprints. Protect the back of the glass with another solid piece of contact paper, or cover the underside edges with masking tape.

MATERIALS

clip glass frame with mat

TOOLS

glass cleaner or vinegar and water solution

vinyl contact paper

stencil or rubber stamp and ink pad

X-Acto knife

Q-tips

rubber gloves

goggles

etching cream

small foam brush

5. Move the glass to a newspaper-covered work area. Wearing rubber gloves and goggles, apply an even, heavy layer of etching cream to the exposed areas of glass with the foam brush. For the best coverage, brush the cream over the edges onto the vinyl paper, using left to right, then top to bottom, strokes.

6. Let the etching cream remain on the glass for the time indicated in the manufacturer's directions, usually about 5 minutes. Wash off the cream in the sink with tap water. When all of the cream has been removed, peel off the vinyl paper to expose the final image. Clean the glass well in warm soapy water. Assemble the clip frame with the mat and artwork.

❖　❖　❖

Like simple clip glass frames, floating glass frames—two pieces of glass front to back—do not compromise the precious beauty of delicate botanical subjects.

frame with silk mat

Don't limit yourself to a wood frame and cardboard mat when highlighting a special image. Fabric coverings are an easy way to bring a new dimension to a frame. Here, the softness of natural suede-covered frames and the elegant sheen of silk mats create lush surroundings for a pair of botanical prints. The fabric colors you choose can be coordinated with the framed image or with other accents in your home. The silk dupioni (raw silk) used to cover the mats adds an interesting note of texture to the frames. Suede is an ideal choice for covering a picture frame because its firm but pliable hand is easy to smooth around the frame's surfaces. Select a lighter weight suede for easier handling.

MATERIALS

flatfaced wooden frame

suede to cover frame

precut mat or chipboard

silk dupioni to cover mat

TOOLS

spray adhesive

rotary cutter

1. Remove the backing materials and glass from the frame. Lay the suede face down and carefully press with an iron to remove any wrinkles. With a ruler and the frame as a guide, cut a rectangle from the suede that is 2 inches larger than the frame all around.

2. Remove the frame; spray the back of the suede with adhesive. Gently position the frame face down in the center of the rectangle and press to adhere. Trim out the approximate 2- by 2-inch squares from each corner of the suede. The inner corner of each square should just touch each outside corner of the frame. Fold one edge of suede onto the side and then the back of the frame, smoothing out the suede as you go. Repeat to fold over the remaining edges. Miter the suede on the back corners of the frame by trimming the overlapping suede diagonally with the rotary cutter.

3. With scissors, snip a hole in the center of the fabric covering the window. Cut diagonally between each set of opposite corners to make an

"X" through the opening, carefully cutting into the corners of the frame. Fold one triangular flap up onto the rabbet and press gently to adhere. Run the rotary cutter along the inside edge to trim off the excess fabric. Repeat for each of the remaining edges.

4. Use a precut mat or make your own by drafting the measurements you want onto the chipboard and then cutting it out. If you cut your own mat, keep in mind that when you are determining its width, allow for about $3/8$ inch on each side of the mat to cover the rabbet overlap.

5. Lay the silk dupioni face down and carefully press with an iron to remove any wrinkles. Cut out a rectangle that is about $1/2$ inch larger than the mat all around. Spray adhesive on the wrong side of the silk, and center the mat on top (face down if the mat is precut), pressing gently to adhere. Turn the mat over and smooth the silk.

6. With scissors, cut an "X" in the center of the fabric covering the window of the mat. Fold each triangular section onto the back of the mat and press to adhere. Trim the points of the triangular sections if they extend beyond the mat.

7. Insert the glass, mat, and artwork to complete the frame.

❖   ❖   ❖

Framed botanical prints make elegant additions to any room, especially when grouped and framed together in a like manner.

Please join us

for a party

to celebrate our wedding

Saturday, September 11

at 5:00 pm

Donald and Terry's house

21 Bridge Street

Westport

R S V P

John and Carol 212.349.0117

wood-carved frame

By creating a simple grain-like pattern with a carving tool and using two colors of paint, you can dress up a plain frame and create a traditionally styled look with a contemporary twist.

1. Remove the backing materials and glass from the frame. If you have no experience using the carving tool, use the back side of the frame to practice some sample strokes, following the direction of the grain. (Don't worry, it's easy!) Apply light, steady pressure with the tip, aiming down slightly as you begin. When you reach a desired length, finish the stroke by angling the tool up slightly, and remove the slice of wood.

2. When you are comfortable with the tool, begin to cover the front of the frame with long, irregular strokes, going with the grain. Fill in one panel at a time and use the mitered joint as a border for the carved strokes on each panel. Repeat to carve the sides of the frame.

3. With the stiff brush, paint the front and sides of the frame with yellow paint. Use the bristles to spread the paint into the carved areas. Let dry. If needed, apply another coat and let dry.

4. With the foam brush, apply a thin coat of white paint to the top surface of the frame. Be sure to wipe all excess paint from the brush before beginning a stroke to prevent paint from running into the carved areas. Let dry. If needed, apply a second coat and let dry. Apply 2 coats of varnish, allowing it to dry between coats.

5. Cut 2 pieces of ribbon 1 inch longer than the mat's height and 2 pieces 1 inch longer than the mat's width. Place the long pieces on the mat vertically, about 1/8 inch from the window. Wrap the ribbons around the mat and glue the ends to the back. Repeat with the short pieces, placing them horizontally across the mat. Insert the glass, mat, artwork, and backing to complete the frame.

MATERIALS

flatfaced unfinished hardwood frame with mat

sunflower yellow acrylic paint

white acrylic paint

matte water-based varnish

ribbon

TOOLS

V-shaped carving tool

stiff paint brush

foam brush

white glue

❖　❖　❖

shadow box frame

A shadow box is a wonderful way to show off that collection of trinkets and odds and ends you've built up over the years. It also makes a heartfelt gift, filled with mementos of times shared. We found most of the items for this travel-themed box at flea markets, antique shows, and garage sales. The shadow box we used came from the craft store with a grid of dividers, with notches cut into them so they would fit together. We used an old map to line the inside of the box, but you can use any other heavy paper or felt.

1. Remove the glass, backboard and dividers from the shadow box. Lightly sand any imperfections or splinters on the frame's edges.

2. Move the frame to a newspaper-covered work surface. With a brush, apply one coat of red paint to the sides and front of the frame. Let dry thoroughly.

3. Dilute the liquid hide glue with water (2 parts glue, 1 part water). With a brush, apply the glue to the frame. Let dry thoroughly. If you would like large cracks in the top coat of paint, use less water when diluting the glue, or use the glue straight from the container. The heavier the application of glue, the larger the cracks will be. Test different dilutions on a separate piece of wood to create the look you like best.

4. With a large brush, apply a coat of turquoise paint to the frame using long, steady strokes. Cracks in the paint will appear almost immediately. Try not to overlap brush strokes, as this would cover over cracks that have formed. Let dry thoroughly, at least 1 or 2 nights.

5. Following manufacturer's directions, spray the shadow box frame with the polyurethane spray. Let dry thoroughly.

6. Cover the backboard with heavyweight paper: Lay the backboard

MATERIALS

11- by 14-inch shadow box with wooden grid of 2 horizontal and 2 vertical dividers

red acrylic paint

turquoise acrylic paint

heavyweight paper and/or felt

foam core

$9/16$- by $1^1/4$-inch brass corners or small brass screws

picture hanger fasteners

TOOLS

fine sandpaper

paint brushes

liquid hide glue, such as Titebond

gloss polyurethane spray

all-purpose craft glue, such as Aleene's "Tacky" glue

X-Acto knife

heavy duty all-purpose contact adhesive in a tube, such as Quick Grab

glass cleaner

on the paper and, with a pencil, trace around the backboard; cut out. Dilute some craft glue with just enough water so it can be easily brushed and apply a thin coat of glue to the front side of the backboard. Carefully lay the back of the paper on the backboard. With the side of your hand, smooth the paper from the center out, pushing out any air bubbles. Let dry.

7. Cover the dividers to hide the notches: Using just the horizontal dividers (save the vertical dividers for another project, or discard), measure and cut 2 pieces of heavyweight paper to go around the top, bottom, and front edge of the dividers. (We used some heavyweight paper here, but you could use more map paper to cover the dividers.) With a brush, apply a thin coat of diluted craft glue to the 3 sides of the dividers and carefully wrap with the paper, smoothing out any air bubbles. Let dry. With the X-Acto knife, trim the edges of the paper so they are just flush with the ends and one long side of each divider. If you like, cut strips from a map and glue on the outside edge as trim, as we have done here.

8. Lay the frame in place on top of the backboard, leaving the glass off. Position your items, including the dividers, in a pleasing fashion. To give the contents more dimension and add interest, you might want to raise some of the flat pieces by gluing a few pieces of foam core behind them, as we did with the 2 circular maps and the "One World" needle case. It may also help to glue small pieces of foam core behind objects that don't lie flat and may be difficult to glue down, like our camera and Statue of Liberty.

9. After everything is arranged to your satisfaction, begin gluing the pieces to the backboard, starting with the dividers. Mark 2 points 3 inches from the top and 2 points 3 inches from the bottom. Draw 2 horizontal lines to use as guides for the dividers. Squeeze a line of contact adhesive to the unpapered long edge of each divider.

Carefully set the dividers in place on the backboard. Let dry.

Use contact adhesive to attach the heavier objects to the backboard and craft glue for the foam core and lighter pieces.

10. The inside of the frame can be painted or lined with more map paper (as we have done here), other heavyweight paper, or felt. To line the inside, measure the sides and cut out pieces, but don't glue them onto the sides until after the glass is in (the glass will not fit correctly if there is excess material).

11. Before gluing the glass into the frame, carefully clean both sides of the glass with glass cleaner. Squeeze small beads of contact adhesive all the way around the inside edge of the frame. Carefully drop the glass into the frame, wiping away any excess glue that oozes out. Place a heavy book inside the frame to weigh down the glass. Allow to dry thoroughly. With a small brush, apply a thin coat of diluted craft glue to the inside surfaces of the frame and carefully position the map paper, smoothing out air bubbles.

12. When everything is thoroughly dry, slip the back of the box into place. To hold the shadow box together, screw on brass corners as we have done here, use small decorative brass screws in the corners, or glue the inner edges together (using contact adhesive). Screw fasteners onto the back of the box for hanging.

■ When painting the shadow box and spraying it with polyurethane, prop the box up with inverted paper cups to keep it from sticking to the newspapers.

■ A hair dryer can be used to speed up the drying time of the paint and glue.

❖　　❖　　❖

chapter three

decorating
with frames

Before you start hanging pictures, first consider the look you want to achieve. Do you want the pictures to dominate, or to blend with their surroundings? Do you feel that you can't have too many pictures, or are you someone who prefers a stark, graphic look? Do you want all the pictures framed alike to give a room a sense of unity, or do you want the framed images to all be different to avoid a mass-produced look?

Assess the space: Try to look at the room with an unbiased, fresh eye. Pretend you're entering it for the first time. What is your immediate impression? Perhaps a large window, ornate moldings, or a high ceiling catches your eye. If so, these are the features you might use as a starting point for arranging pictures. Pictures raise the visual level of interest in a room and this can increase the impression of height, even in a low-ceilinged space. Are there wall areas that are completely blank? Bring them into the foreground with a dynamic grouping of pictures. Do pictures seem to float aimlessly on the walls? Consider pushing a sofa or table against the wall to use as an anchor for the group of pictures above. Bring vitality to a forgotten corner by gracing it with a small grouping of charming pictures. By adding focal points to a room, you give it an identity.

If the room has paneling or pronounced woodwork, think of it as an extra dimension of framing. You'll find that the room often suggests its own solutions. Listen to your eyes.

Placement

Though everyone seems to have an individual theory on picture placement, there's a certain irrefutable logic as to which pictures should go where. For instance, large paintings need large rooms, so that you can step back to view them properly and so that they don't seem cramped on the wall. Landscapes of even moderate size also need extra space for the viewer to see them in the right perspective. To show them off at eye level, position them about five feet from the floor. On the other hand, bear in mind that eye level will change once you're seated, to about 48 to 53 inches, so consider from what position the art is most likely to be viewed.

Tiny spaces such as hallways or spare rooms call for small-scale art works, which need to be seen up close to be fully appreciated. By the same token, when deciding how to blend assorted sizes of pictures together, place the smaller ones lower down so that they can be enjoyed at eye level or below. Larger paintings will also have the effect of drawing attention to smaller ones. But never underestimate the power of the unexpected placement: A pair or a trio of smaller pictures are more powerful and capture the eye when hung over a door, on a landing, or in an odd-shaped corner. Or highlight a smaller picture by pairing it with an oversize mat and frame.

Decorating with pictures can be a delicate balancing act. Strong paintings overpower subtle ones, and even one another; if a collection of powerful paintings is hung too closely together, the effect will be overwhelming. The goal is a gentle integration of styles.

Pictures earn their keep as much as any other furnishing. When it comes to correcting proportion problems in rooms, most of us turn to paint or wallpaper first. But clever arrangements of pictures can have an equally profound—and quick—cosmetic effect. If the ceilings are too high, bring them down to earth with horizontal arrangements, perhaps using a trompe l'oeil motif, such as painted ivy

Pastoral engravings in bamboo-look frames conjure English country house elegance. Placed just above the couch and expanding the wall space, they comfortably meet the seated viewer's eye while echoing the shape of the windows above.

to trail from ceiling to wall to paintings, to lead the eye downward. Rooms with low ceilings often benefit from pictures stacked in vertical arrangements, practically touching the ceiling, which creates the illusion of height. However, keep in mind that a low-ceilinged room that is also small can seem crowded if the walls are completely covered with pictures. Again, balance is the key.

Room by Room

Traditionally, people display their most important pictures in the living room, but there are many other opportunities throughout the house to hang art.

The entry hall is where first impressions are made, so it is a perfect place for showing off jewel-like smaller pieces of your collection. Ornately framed mirrors are also right at home here, providing the illusion of a larger space.

Pictures can also enliven staircases. One option is to stack pictures in vertical rows. Another is to completely cover the walls from floor to ceiling with disparate shapes and sizes; keeping in mind that larger pictures look

better higher up. Yet a third approach is to create a kind of horizontal continuity by having the framed artwork ascend at eye level or slightly above. To avoid a dizzying effect, keep the spacing between the pictures consistent.

Artwork displayed in the kitchen helps to keep the room from having a strictly utilitarian feel. For instance, framed contemporary needlepoint or a textile such as a quilt block could decorate the walls of a breakfast area, perhaps harmonizing with the colors of china displayed in a plate rack. Such tactile images bring a softness to the hard edges of a kitchen. Shadow box collections and framed decoupage art are also perfect here.

The bathroom is a wonderful spot to display copies of family pictures (keep the originals safely away from heat and humidity) or old class photos from the flea market. Don't overlook the possibility of hanging a surprise picture inside a closet or cupboard door.

If you have a guest room that you would like to double as a sitting room or library, consider giving it that classic English print room feel with pictures hung floor to ceiling.

To lend character to a home office or family room, theme it to a pursuit or interest. Take your collection of antique buttons or baseball cards out of the tissue paper and use it to dramatize the walls in shadow box or Plexiglas frames.

One room can borrow a view from the other: Seen through a doorway, a series of identically matted and framed snapshots turns an ordinary wall into a focal point. In the foreground on a pine cupboard, strong, graphic photographs play off the profile of a fluted bowl.

Grouping

The grouping of framed images can be a daunting task—how to organize it all?—but there are some guidelines that will make it easier. First sort your pictures by shape, style, or color. This will help avoid "spotty picture hanging technique," in which pictures are scattered hither and thither, rather than grouped together to create the greatest impact. For instance, portraits facing each other or flanking paintings will create a resonant effect and even seem to be interacting. If you're grouping works with similar subject matter by different artists—for instance, flowers in a basket—the overarching theme will create affinities between the images even if the artistic techniques are quite different.

Begin by laying out a group of pictures on the floor and moving them around like playing cards to create a balanced arrangement. By doing this, you'll be able to plan the desired effect before you even pick up a hammer.

With the artwork on the floor, keep these guidelines in mind: If you're bringing many differently shaped frames together, perhaps interspersing them with objects such as antique Staffordshire platters, arrange the whole in a shape, like a triangle or circle. Place the largest piece at center, and build outward from there. Don't hesitate to mix ovals, rectangles, and squares within the overall grouping.

Compare the measurements of the final result with the wall itself to make sure it actually fits, then record your arrangement in a notepad. Transfer the design to the wall using light pencil marks to designate hanging spots. Maintain consistent spacing between the individual pieces, to keep the eye moving rhythmically around the composition.

Alternatively, you can design around imaginary latitudes and longitudes in the room. Designate a horizontal axis—an equator—that serves as a guideline for hanging pictures above or below. Mark it lightly on the wall using a pencil. If you hang the pictures with their tops or bottoms aligned above or below the line, the effect will be clean lined, graphic, and contemporary. If you center each picture individually along the line—that is, each picture's length is equally divided above and below—the look will be more traditional.

At the same time, several vertical axes would be helpful for hanging groups of pictures from floor to ceiling. Avoid a rigid column effect by varying the shapes and sizes of these vertically oriented pictures, perhaps a large picture above a smaller oval rising on

Hung to fit within a stairway's woodwork molding, mirrors reflect light from an adjacent window and throw it back into the house. Their intriguingly carved frames encourage visitors to slow down and examine them, along with the collection of early garden sprinklers on the steps.

the wall over a chair whose carving, fabric, or painted details harmonize with the art above. If an arrangement is pleasing to your eye, even if it bucks common decorating wisdom, go with it—sometimes the most unusual solutions are the best.

Perhaps the most common pitfall in living, dining, and bedroom areas is hanging art too high. In general, place it three or four inches lower than your perception of eye level. If you're hanging art in a room where people will be seated for the most part, hang pictures just about five or six inches above couch level. In hallways, eye level art or even a bit higher

works best—to protect it from passersby.

If you are hanging an image over a large focal point—a couch or long table—smaller groupings can add up to big impact. The grouping doesn't have to echo the traditional rectangular lines of the couch or table: instead, create a pyramid or a circle as a counterpoint.

Tricks of the Trade

In addition to the basic picture hanging guidelines, there are certain tricks for making framed images work in a room. The common assumption is that pictures work best in odd numbered groups, which are naturally harmonious to the eye because they always provide a central position, or focal point. For instance, trios often look right, whether hung horizontally or vertically. Museums often follow the odd-numbered formula, positioning the most important work at center—perhaps a central horizontal flanked by two verticals, which in turn are bordered by two horizontal paintings—all smaller than the middle picture.

Of course, clever groupings of even numbers also succeed, and they can create a

Left: This odd-numbered picture arrangement draws on two grouping formulas—horizontals are flanked by verticals, arranged within a deliberately imperfect square. Everything is positioned in relation to the central image. Opposite: A quartet of flower photographs stacked in pairs adds calm geometry to a bath wall.

calming, ordered effect—especially when it comes to prints, photographs, and posters with related themes or colors. Try stacking one picture over another—hanging a smaller one beneath a larger one invites inspection of the bottom piece of art. Conversely, hanging the smaller one on top has a more pleasingly balanced feel. Or work in quartets arranged in a square or rectangle, perhaps mixing genuine antique botanical prints with new images cut from a calendar. With clever presentation—identical or similar frames and mats—the rare ones will seem friendlier; the store-bought ones more refined. Hang them in either a straight line—perhaps from a picture rail—or two up, two down in a block.

An even-numbered grouping can be turned into an odd simply with the addition of a wild card element, whether a central mirror or an architectural carving. For example, placing an oval mirror between two pictures creates intrigue while reinforcing the sense of symmetry.

There is also merit in the seemingly spontaneous arrangement, which is comforting in its informality. Asymmetry can give a room a one-of-a-kind personality.

When hanging a hodgepodge of prints, posters, or other art, using similar mats or frames adds cohesion. Painted details on the wall itself can also unite a varied grouping, such as trompe l'oeil painted ribbons that tie the pictures together or, if the framed material has a nautical or western theme, a rope motif.

One decorator trick is to place pictures on a wall opposite a mirror. In this way, your perception of the groupings changes depending on where you stand in the room. When you see pictures reflected in the mirror, they become an arrangement on that wall.

When wall space is at a minimum, hang pictures directly on a door. This is also a good way of camouflaging a doorway in a small room where you want to extend the walls visually.

Hanging Considerations

To minimize the damage that hanging pictures does to your walls, use tiny tungsten steel nails or picture hooks. If you truly can't bear to put holes in the walls, add a picture rail and use traditional brass hooks to hang pictures by wire or decorative cord. Keep in mind that this method makes sense only if you want to hang pictures in a row, albeit in varying heights. With picture hanging systems available at specialty frame shops, you have the option of hanging several pictures along one vertical rod.

Many frame shops place hangers a third of the way down the height of picture, which makes the picture tilt forward slightly. Of course, canting a frame forward—as the Victorians were so fond of doing—has its merits. It allows a picture to lean into the room, which is effective when artwork is hung up high. This is a particularly intriguing way of showing off portraits.

If you want your art to lie flat, come less than a third of the way down the length of the picture when placing hangers: The higher up they are, the flatter the picture lies.

When you're stringing wire across the back of a frame between two hangers, make sure it hangs in a gentle arc. If pulled too tightly between the hangers, it will generate a much greater force, approximately eight times the weight of the picture, and possibly pull the nail out of the wall.

Anything frameable that measures more than 8 by 14 inches or weighs more than ten pounds needs extra stability. Balance the picture by adding screws or nails to the wall so that the picture can be supported on both sides. This way, it can hang on two separate wires or picture chains, which distribute the weight evenly.

When it comes to especially bulky items like mirrors, don't use wire at all. Instead, suspend them from two nails or screws on 'D' rings screwed into the frame.

With stone or brick walls, you have two options. Drive a masonry nail into the mortar and use to hang the picture. Or drill into the wall using a masonry bit and insert a plastic or wooden anchor; screw the picture hook into that and hang a picture by means of cord or chain. Many specialty frame shops—for instance, those affiliated with the Professional Picture Framers Association—carry traditional velvet-covered cord for a more attractive effect, and many decorators (and do-it-yourselfers) have been known to custom-cover cord with fabric.

These handtinted 19th-century Pierre-Joseph Redouté botanical prints have an orderly yet unstudied air. Though the picture alignment is somewhat random, green mats and gold frames lend unity to the group, while linking it to the chair rail below.

The Single Image

As satisfying as it is to arrange frames in groups, sometimes an image is so powerful that it should be left on its own. It might be a particularly compelling portrait in a heavy gilt frame—so powerful it can only be displayed by itself against a pale backdrop. Or it could be a contemporary or abstract work of art whose colors and subject simply don't mix easily with anything else. In this case, consider a bold, deep, stylish frame, perhaps one of ebonized wood with stepped-out corners—and leave plenty of blank wall space around it for maximum impact. If the image is so powerful it barely seems to be contained on the canvas, perhaps no frame is needed at all.

If you want to call attention to a single image, hang it between doorways. If your home has a built-in architectural feature such as a niche, take advantage of it. Any painting hung there will be naturally highlighted. Or place a piece of framed artwork so that it is visible through a doorway and is the first thing you see upon entering a room.

Another way of making a big statement is to hang a series of prints of a single subject—architectural drawings or watercolors of interiors, for instance—frame to frame, virtually touching, which creates the bold effect of one large picture.

Flexible Arrangements

An anonymous painting from the early 17th century called *Cognoscenti in a Room Hung with Pictures* reveals much about how displaying pictures has changed over the years. The picture shows a room with paintings hung floor to ceiling, fit in jigsawlike on every available surface and even propped against furniture. There's a very temporary feeling to the arrangement, as if it would all look different if you came back ten minutes later. The painting is an excellent record of a time when pictures were meant to be portable, not fixed, as they were intended to be taken down for close enjoyment.

Collectors are rediscovering the pleasures of this more flexible arrangement of pictures. It makes perfect sense to place paintings where they're accessible, on shelves and table-tops, easels, mantels, or dangling from cupboard doors. Prop paintings on chairs or on pedestals as surprise treats for the eye. Installing a narrow picture shelf on your wall will allow you to easily move pictures around, without making any nail holes. When

With its frame painted in bold awning stripes, a lighthouse painting becomes a beacon to the eye. Its unusual position on a bookcase further draws attention and invites the viewer to study the collectibles perched on the shelves, a plaid tin forties picnic basket and handpainted lighthouse model among them.

something stays in one place for too long, you stop seeing it. Instead, think of your framed art as dynamic pieces that can move from room to room, house to house, always giving their surroundings a fresh new look. And if you ever outgrow a picture, don't be afraid to consign it to auction or barter with a friend.

Art of the Tableau

Picturesque groupings of related or unrelated objects sprinkled around a framed work give it a new dimension. This technique is called the art of the tableau, and there are infinite variations.

Here's how it works: Place a provincial milk pitcher filled with sweet peas alongside an oil painting of a field of flowers in a floridly carved frame and suddenly the picture seems more accessible, less formal. But pair that same painting with a symmetrical arrangement of gold candlesticks and you get a quite different, somewhat decorous, effect. A line drawing of a woman's face displayed next to a carved wooden bust and a stack of colorful portfolios conveys a strong artistic theme. The same drawing arranged with an antique vanity set and pair of gloves creates a feminine vignette.

Just as frames and mats heighten or soften particular colors in a piece of art, objects in the immediate vicinity do the same. A painting with deep, rich colors displayed alongside translucent porcelain provides visual relief and contrast. Muted colors of a seashore painting are reinforced by buff-colored salt-glaze stoneware. A tablescape of black and white objects gathered around a simple black and white engraving draws attention to the graphic appeal of what otherwise might have been an overlooked piece of art.

When carefully chosen, objects can help pictures come to life. Juxtapose a stack of books with worn leather bindings with a historical painting and you've enriched the sense of the past. Set a bowl of fruit before a still-life of oranges and the imagery will seem to leap off the canvas.

Tableaux can also tell tales. A portrait of a lady with an ambiguous expression invites all sorts of story lines. You could introduce a framed photograph of a man propped on the table below, or you might pair her with fine silver, such as biscuit jars and footed tea trays, to evoke an Edith Wharton–ish type of tale. A primitive painting of an American homestead could be surrounded by handmade farm tools, a tole document box and mug, and carved

Scalloped-edge shelves support a series of contemporary fern prints, displayed side by side with similarly styled china plates.

Because they are not affixed to a wall, the pictures can easily migrate to another room—or move aside to make way for more.

painted wall. One English custom is to hang prints and paintings directly on bookshelves. Not only is this a wonderful solution for rooms such as libraries, where every square inch may already be taken up by books, but it is a simple way to add a rich layer of decoration and to break up the monotony of the books themselves. Hang the pictures at eye level from the upright supports of the shelves or just prop them among the shelves.

Many people hesitate to display art against wallpaper. By all means, go right ahead; if you are unsure about whether something will work, limit the subject matter to something fairly simple, such as portraits or architectural drawings. Make the mats oversize to provide a strong visual break from the backdrop. A two-toned double mat is a good example: a pale inner mat, perhaps ornamented with a washline, contained within a slightly darker outer mat. The frames should also be broad. So, too, this is an opportunity to show off a truly beautiful frame with no image within as an art piece. At the same time, the frame should generally relate to the wallpaper—that is, you wouldn't pair a

objects such as whistles or walking sticks, all of which the viewer might pleasantly imagine to be artifacts of daily life magically extracted from the picture.

Backgrounds

Long ago in English homes, pictures were hung on tapestries. While no one today would poke holes in a handmade textile, you should consider taking a more creative approach to showing off framed images, beyond the

Flowering vine wallpaper proves a tranquil background for a dreamy landscape. Crystal lamps and candlesticks aren't arranged here in a chance tableau—their light-reflecting facets make the gilt frame seem to glitter all the more.

chrome frame with a delicate floral print.

Never shy away from working with brick and stone: Rough textured walls can enhance the polished brilliance of a formal frame, or serve as a handsome, rustic backdrop for the simplest Early American–style frames of black-painted wood.

If you're starting fresh in a new home and have the luxury of painting the walls to suit your picture collection, play with paint chips to get the right effect. For an image that is particularly striking, paint the walls a color that complements the frame, mat color, or the artwork itself. Take a tip from museums: If you'll be showing off a particularly imposing, deep-toned picture, choose a neutral color as a backdrop, such as olive green, warm gray, gray-blue, or paper-bag brown. White tempered by a hint of brown to reduce glare also works nicely.

Perhaps neutral shades are too tame for your taste: Go ahead and make a bold color statement. Many lighter colored paintings such as softly defined watercolors look wonderful against rich reddish brown or hunter green walls. When you use bold colors as a background, you can repeat them in the mat for a cohesive look. The absence of color in a painting also lends itself to vibrant walls. For instance, simple black and white drawings benefit enormously from the contrast of a backdrop of mustard yellow or apricot walls.

The guidelines for framing come down to a simple precept—keep an open mind. As you determine how to frame artwork and where to hang it, pay attention to proportion, scale, color, and tone, but don't feel wedded to someone else's rules. What and how you decide to frame is ultimately your decision, especially when you consider that in a world full of mass-produced items, frames can introduce a truly personal touch into your home. As long as you follow your instincts and decorate to please your eyes alone, keeping to your own aesthetic sense, the results will lend character and interest to any room.

collections on display

Consider these ideas for showing off collections, both flat and three-dimensional, and creating interesting arrangements:

Antique clothing

- Children's and vintage doll's clothing, ribbons, beaded scarves and gloves, lace collars, vests, and belts can be framed flat or in shadow boxes.
- Fabric can work as matting to ornament a frame. Secure a complementary pattern to the backing with a needle and thread or dressmaker's pins, place an image over it, and add the glass and frame.
- Look inside thrift shop clothing for beautiful old embroidered labels, which, when placed in small wide-matted frames, can be more interesting than the clothing they accompanied.

Samplers, needlepoint, and other textiles

- Enhance the effect of framed fabric even further by adding to the sewing theme. Place a needle- and thimble-case collection or a collection of buttons in jars on a table in the foreground. Framed buttons can also take their place on the wall alongside textiles: display in shadow box frames grouped by color—for instance, black and white—and juxtapose a wide variety of shapes such as trefoils, ovals, and bars in symmetrical rows. Use an interesting, complementary fabric as backing.
- Especially when the needlework has a message, theme it to the room. For instance, a pair of pillow shams featuring red turkeywork stitchery that read "Good Night" and "Good Morning" are pretty on a bedroom wall.

Travel

- Vintage maps, framed with richly colored mats, look wonderful displayed with a collection of old globes.
- Maritime maps and nautical prints are natural partners for model clipper ships, antique binoculars, barometers, and scrimshaw.
- Linen-finish vintage postcards (many of them tinted by hand) look great framed in groups of three or more for a whimsical touch in a bathroom or hallway. Also frame "souvenir folders," which fold out with various views of a particular place. One side is usually horizontal and the other vertical—consider a clip glass frame for a view of both sides.
- Framed ticket stubs, wine labels, and restaurant menus keep a special vacation always in mind. A multi-windowed mat can show off a collection of unusual matchbooks.

Western and Native Americana

- Old magazine covers featuring cowboys look great on a wall alongside a collection of hats.
- Native American portraits from old calendars stand out in beaded frames on a table covered with a Southwestern-style fabric.
- Arrowheads make vivid geometric artwork when sheltered in a deep frame.

Sporting paraphernalia

- A catcher's mitt, autographed ball, and scorecards framed together in a shadow box is a nice addition to a young fan's room.
- Beautiful old fishing gear such as lures or flies, sewn in place on a mat, and reels, anchored with

fishing line, are wonderful shadow box subjects.

- Autographed baseball cards can be preserved for posterity in a frame decorated with souvenir bats.

Fruits and flowers

- Group images of one kind of flower (roses or peonies), fruit, or theme (pictures of flowers in baskets) and display with vases filled with fresh-picked bouquets in the foreground.
- Hang flower pictures alongside real flowers in vintage ceramic wall pockets. Bowls, pillows, curtains, and hooked rugs with floral motifs are also natural display companions.

Animal themes

- To enhance framed Audubon prints (or look-alikes), cluster a few birdhouses old or new on a table below.
- Many collectors amass single animals—rabbits, elephants, cows, or pigs, for example—and supplement their collection with framed illustrations from children's books.
- Group dog or cat portraits with dog or cat figurines. Amateur portraits of pets can often be found in flea markets.

Fruit and vegetables

- Shawnee corn-theme cookie jars and serving ware from the forties, apple-shaped cookie jars, and salt and pepper shakers with garden themes are fun collectibles to harmonize with framed seed catalogs, vintage seed packets, or herb tin labels.
- Painted still-lifes of bowls of fruit are attractive hung with a mix of floral patterned plates.

Calligraphy and typography

- What might today be considered mundane documents used to be highly decorated. Framing them brings their artistry to life: pages from a Victorian ledger, old bank notes, invoices with unusual letterheads, deeds with elaborate scrollwork.
- Old advertisements from the twenties and thirties, food labels from the forties—indeed, any colorful or unusual packaging—can be paired with other images from their era (McCoy pottery, for example) to create a look that takes you back in time.
- Framing a marriage certificate is a timeless way to mark an important milestone.

Childhood pursuits

- Shadow boxes are the perfect foil for children's collections. Use them to display the discoveries—butterflies or beautifully colored insects—of a budding naturalist. Children's play things such as wood blocks, game pieces, tin toys, dollhouse furniture, and playing cards can fill up the compartments of a shadow box painted in a bright primary color.
- Next to a photo of a joyful child on Christmas morning, perhaps set in a red and green plaid fabric frame, arrange snow domes and snowmen ornaments collected over the years.

index

Acknowledgments

The author would like to thank:

The Professional Picture Framers Association; William Parker, CPF,
Ambience by Parker Incorporated, Nashville, Tennessee; Jack and Beth Devine,
Spook Hill Frames, Wappingers Falls, New York; Art Ungar, Photo Restoring
by Art, Lawrenceville, New Jersey; Margy Norrish, Cinnamon Studio, Groton,
Massachusetts; North End Fabrics, Boston, Massachusetts

Frame on page 48 by Ella Hudson
Frames and how-to instructions on pages 51, 52, 55, 59, 63, 67, 71, 72,
75, 79, and 83 by Mary Ann Hall and Sandra Salamony
Frame and how-to instructions on page 84 by Karen Silver Bloom